HIDING IN

FORESTS

Deborah Underwood

Heinemann Library
Chicago, Illinois

H www.heinemannraintree.com
Visit our website to find out more information about Heinemann-Raintree books.

To order:

☎ Phone 888-454-2279

💻 Visit www.heinemannraintree.com to browse our catalog and order online.

Edited by Rebecca Rissman and Nancy Dickmann
Designed by Joanna Hinton Malivoire
Picture research by Tracy Cummins
Originated by Capstone Global Library
Printed and bound in China by Leo Paper Products Ltd

15 14 13 12 11
10 9 8 7 6 5 4 3 2 1

Library of Congress Cataloging-in-Publication Data
Underwood, Deborah.
  Hiding in forests / Deborah Underwood. -- 1st ed.
      p. cm. -- (Creature camouflage)
  Includes bibliographical references and index.
  ISBN 978-1-4329-4022-5 (hc) -- ISBN 978-1-4329-4031-7 (pb) 1. Forest animals--Juvenile literature. 2. Camouflage (Biology)--Juvenile literature. I. Title.
  QL112.U53 2010
  591.47'2--dc22
                              2009051765

Acknowledgments
The author and publisher are grateful to the following for permission to reproduce copyright material: Getty Images pp. 6 (David Tipling), 9 (altrendo nature), 11, 12 (Panoramic Images), 15, 16 (Ben Hall), 19, 20 (Gary Buss), 21, 22 (Mattias Klum); Minden Pictures pp. 17, 18 (Nature Production/Seiichi Meguro); naturepl.com pp. 23, 24 (© Staffan Widstrand), 25, 26 (© Rachel Hingley); Photolibrary pp. 13, 14 (Oxford Scientific (OSF); Shutterstock pp. 4 (© SNEHIT), 5 (© Alexandru Axon), 7 (© Brian Dunne), 8 (© Sascha Burkard), 10 (© Rusty Dodson), 27 (© Smirnof), 28 (© Ronnie Howard), 29 (© blind shot).

Cover photograph of a tawny owl (Strix aluco) in a tree trunk reproduced with permission of naturepl.com (© David Tipling).

We would like to thank Michael Bright for his invaluable help in the preparation of this book.

Every effort has been made to contact copyright holders of any material reproduced in this book. Any omissions will be rectified in subsequent printings if notice is given to the publisher.

All the Internet addresses (URLs) given in this book were valid at the time of going to press. However, due to the dynamic nature of the Internet, some addresses may have changed, or sites may have changed or ceased to exist since publication. While the author and publisher regret any inconvenience this may cause readers, no responsibility for any such changes can be accepted by either the author or the publisher.

Contents

Some words are printed in bold, **like this**. You can find out what they mean by looking in the glossary.

What Are Forests Like?

Forests are places where trees are the main type of plant. There are different types of forests. **Boreal forests** have trees with needle-shaped leaves.

Most trees with needle-shaped leaves do not change color.

The trees in some forests have leaves that change color.

The animals in this book live in **temperate forests**. These forests have four **seasons**. Most trees in temperate forests lose their leaves in the fall.

Living in a Forest

Many kinds of animals live in a forest. Some forest animals have special body **features** to help them **survive**. These features are called **adaptations**.

Woodpeckers use their strong beaks to dig nest holes in forest trees.

Black bears eat fruit, nuts, and honey. They also hunt other animals.

Some animals survive by eating other animals. These animals are called **predators**. The animals they eat are called **prey**.

What Is Camouflage?

Camouflage (KAM-uh-flaj) is an **adaptation** that helps animals hide. The color of an animal's skin, fur, or feathers may match the things around it.

This squirrel's brown fur matches the tree.

A green luna moth on a tree looks like a leaf.

The shape of an animal may camouflage it, too. Some animals are shaped like sticks or leaves. Why do you think animals need to hide?

Some **predators** hide so they can sneak up on **prey** animals. Prey animals hide so they won't become a predator's lunch!

This copperhead snake's brown colors help it hide in dead leaves.

Find the Forest Animals

Bobcat

The bobcat is a type of cat that lives in northern forests. Bobcats hunt and eat other animals. Their fur color helps them hide as they hunt.

CAMOUFLAGED

Bobcats eat small animals, such as squirrels and birds. Some bobcats also hunt bigger animals, such as deer. After they sneak up on **prey**, they pounce!

REVEALED

Spotted owlet

Spotted owlets have feathers that **blend in** with tree **bark**. This **camouflage** helps them hide from larger birds that might eat them.

Spotted owlets mainly hunt at night. An owl sits quietly on a tree branch. When a small animal passes below, the owl swoops down and grabs it!

Roe deer

Adult roe deer have reddish-brown coats in summer. Can you see how a deer's coat helps it hide in the forest? In winter, the deer grow gray or brown coats.

Young roe deer are called fawns. Their coats are brown with light spots. A fawn lies on the ground while its mother looks for food. The spots help the fawn **blend in** with the forest floor.

Siberian flying squirrel

Siberian flying squirrels have coats that change colors, too. They become silver-gray in winter. This makes it harder for **predators** to see them in the snow.

CAMOUFLAGED

Flying squirrels glide through the air. They have flaps of skin between their front and back legs. When the squirrels jump from trees, the flaps catch the wind.

REVEALED

Northern walking stick

If you want to hide in a tree, it helps to look like a stick! Walking sticks are insects. Their shape and color gives them great **camouflage**.

When walking sticks sense danger, they stay very still. This makes them look even more like real sticks.

REVEALED

Gray wolf

The color of gray wolves' coats can help them hide as they hunt. Wolves live in groups called packs. A wolf pack hunts together.

The color of wolves' coats depends partly on where they live. Wolves that live in snowy places may have whiter coats. This helps to **camouflage** them when they hunt.

REVEALED

CAMOUFLAGED

Tawny frogmouth

The tawny (TAW-nee) frogmouth is a type of bird. It lives in parts of Australia. The bird's gray and brown feathers **blend in** with the trees. This helps protect it from **predators**.

23

At night the tawny frogmouth hunts for insects, worms, and other food. During the day, the bird sits in a tree and stays very still. When it closes its eyes and points its head up, it looks like a broken branch!

REVEALED

Peppered moth

A peppered moth on a tree trunk can be very hard to spot! Black and white wings help the moths hide from birds that want to eat them.

A female moth lays eggs. The eggs hatch into caterpillars. Peppered moth caterpillars are good at hiding, too. They look like twigs!

REVEALED

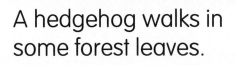

A hedgehog walks in some forest leaves.

If you visit a forest, look closely among the leaves and branches. You may see all sorts of animals hiding there!

Animals that Stand Out

Some forest animals don't hide. Their colors make them stand out. A male cardinal (CAR-dih-nuhl) bird has a bright red color. This helps him attract a female.

A red male cardinal stands out in the green of the forest.

This ladybug's bright color warns other animals not to eat it.

Ladybugs can make a bad smell if another animal tries to eat them. Their bright color warns **predators** to stay away!

Glossary

adaptation special feature that helps an animal survive in its surroundings

bark tough, outer part of a tree trunk

blend in matches well with the things around it

boreal forest forest with long winters and trees with needle-shaped leaves, such as pine trees

camouflage adaptation that helps an animal blend in with the things around it

feature special part of an animal

predator animal that eats other animals

prey animal that other animals eat

seasons parts of the year that have different weather, such as spring, summer, fall, winter

survive stay alive

temperate forest forest that has four seasons

Find Out More

Books to read

Galko, Francine. *Forest Animals*. Chicago: Heinemann Library, 2002.

Ward, Jennifer, and Jamichael Henterly (illustrator). *Forest Bright, Forest Night*. Nevada City, CA: Dawn Publications, 2005.

Websites

www.defenders.org/wildlife_and_habitat/habitat/forest.php
Defenders of Wildlife forest habitat information

www.mbgnet.net/sets/temp/index.htm
Missouri Botanical Garden forest information

www.nps.gov/webrangers/
National Park Service Junior Ranger program

Index